TOILETRIVIA

POP CULTURE

The only trivia book that caters to your everyday bathroom needs

by Jeremy Klaff & Harry Klaff

This book might contain product names, trademarks, or registered trademarks. All trademarks in this book are property of their respective owners. If used, they are for non-biased use, and we do not encourage or discourage use of said product or service. Any term suspected of being a trademark will be properly capitalized.

Cover art by Stephanie Strack

About the Authors

Harry Klaff covered the NHL for *The Hockey News* and *Hockey Pictorial*, and reported for both the Associated Press and United Press International. He has written three books, *All Time Greatest Super Bowl*, *All Time Greatest Stanley Cup*, and *Computer Literacy and Use*.

Today, he is a retired Social Studies teacher from Brooklyn. Because he never went on a date in his adolescence, Harry had plenty of time to research useless facts and figures on everything ranging from history to pop culture. Moonlighting as a hockey scoreboard operator and baseball beer vendor, Harry had ample time to collect data.

Yet somehow, he got married. In 1977, Jeremy was born. Rather than being raised on a steady diet of carrots and peas, baby Jeremy was forced to learn facts from textbooks. His first word was "Uzbekistan." Throughout his childhood, Jeremy had a hard time making friends. When other kids wanted to play baseball, he wanted to instruct them about Henry VIII's six wives. After a failed career as a standup comic and broadcaster, in 2000 Jeremy fittingly became a Social Studies teacher. Today he brings trivia to the next generation.

Collect All Toiletrivia Titles

US History

World History

Pop Culture

Sports

Baseball

Music

and more!

Get the full list of titles at
www.toiletrivia.com

Acknowledgements

We at Toiletrivia would like to thank all of the people who made this possible.

- •The ancient cities of Harappa and Mohenjo Daro for engineering advances in plumbing.

- •Sir John Harrington for inventing the modern flush toilet.

- •Seth Wheeler for his patent of perforated toilet paper.

- •Jeffrey Gunderson for inventing the plunger.

We would like to thank our families for suffering through nights of endless trivia.

We would also like to thank the friendly commuters at the Grand Central Station restroom facility for field testing these editions.

Introduction

Here at *Toiletrivia* we do extensive research on what you, the bathroom user, wish to see in your reading material. Sure, there are plenty of fine books out there to pass the time, but none of them cater to your competitive needs. That's why *Toiletrivia* is here to provide captivating trivia that allows you to interact with fellow bathroom users.

Each chapter allows you to keep score so you can evaluate your progress if you choose to go through the book multiple times. Or, you may wish to leave the book behind for others to play and keep score against you. Perhaps you just want to make it look like you are a genius, and leave a perfect scorecard for all to see. We hope you leave one in every bathroom of the house.

The rules of *Toiletrivia* are simple. Each chapter has 30 questions divided into three sections...One Roll, Two Rolls, or Three Rolls. The One Rolls are easiest and worth one point. Two Rolls are a bit harder and are worth two points. And of course, Three Rolls are the hardest, and are worth three points. You will tabulate your progress on the scorecard near the end of the book.

The questions we have selected are meant for dinner conversation, or impressing people you want to date. With few exceptions, our queries are geared for the uncomfortable situations that life throws at you, like when you have nothing in common with someone, and need to offer some clever banter. We hope that the facts you learn in the restroom make it easier to meet your future in-laws, or deal with that hairdresser who just won't stop talking to you.

Remember, *Toiletrivia* is a game. No joysticks, no computer keyboards...just you, your toilet, and a pen; the way nature intended it. So good luck. We hope you are triumphant.

DIRECTIONS

Each set of questions has an answer sheet opposite it. Write your answers in the first available column to the right. When you are done with a set of 10 questions, *fold* your answer column underneath so the next restroom user doesn't see your answers. *Special note to restroom users 2 and 3: No cheating! And the previous person's answers might be wrong!*

Then check your responses with the answer key in the back of the book. Mark your right answers with a check, and your wrong answers with an "x." Then go to the scorecard on pages 98-100 and tabulate your results. These totals will be the standard for other users to compare.

Be sure to look online for other Toiletrivia titles
Visit us at www.toiletrivia.com

Table of Contents

Television Sitcoms

 ## One Roll

Flip to pg. 68 for answers

1. What is the longest running sitcom in TV history? Funny, the characters haven't aged one bit.

2. In one of the most famous scenes in TV history, what were Lucy and Ethel attempting to put into wrappers on the conveyer belt on *I Love Lucy*?

3. What did Al Bundy do for a living?

4. *Who's the Boss*?

5. What famous actor and future director played Opie on *The Andy Griffith Show*?

6. What classic TV character's chair is now on display at the Smithsonian?

7. Where did Ralph Kramden want to send Alice?

8. Who was the center square of *The Brady Bunch*?

9. What sitcom would you be watching if you saw some of the biggest TV and future movie stars of the 1970s and 1980s working for the Sunshine Cab Company?

10. What famous American sitcom was set in Korea? The series was based on a novel.

Answer Sheet
Television Sitcoms
1 Roll

Name_____

Answer Sheet
Television Sitcoms
1 Roll

Name_____

Answer Sheet
Television Sitcoms
1 Roll

Name_____

1.	1.	1.
2.	2.	2.
3.	3.	3.
4.	4.	4.
5.	5.	5.
6.	6.	6.
7.	7.	7.
8.	8.	8.
9.	9.	9.
10.	10.	10.

After you have filled out the sheet, fold your column underneath along the dashed line so the next restroom user won't see your answers. *The first player uses the far right column.*

Notes:

Notes:

Notes:

Television Sitcoms

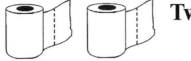

Two Rolls

Flip to pg. 69 for answers

1. What town does Peter Griffin live in?

2. What show's opening sequence includes a glove resting on a moving beer bottle?

3. What legendary sitcom about a dry cleaner on the East Side of New York was a spinoff of another sitcom set in Queens?

4. The best of friends, Felix and Oscar couldn't be more different. That's probably why they were known as this.

5. Liz Sheridan played Jerry Seinfeld's mother on *Seinfeld*. A few years earlier, she also played Mrs. Ochmonek on what TV show about an alien from the planet Melmac?

6. Everyone remembers Urkel. But do you remember the name of the TV show that he debuted on?

7. Pat Morita was known to most as Mr. Miyagi. But to older audiences, he was the owner of Arnold's on what famous sitcom?

8. What President did Alex P. Keaton idolize? He even had this President on his lunchbox!

9. Name two of the three housekeepers for Mr. Drummond on *Diff'rent Strokes*.

10. What crossword-loving worker from *The Office* only likes coming to work on the day they give out free pretzels?

Answer Sheet

Television Sitcoms
2 Rolls

Name_____

1.	
2.	
3.	
4.	
5.	
6.	
7.	
8.	
9.	
10.	

Answer Sheet

Television Sitcoms
2 Rolls

Name_____

1.	
2.	
3.	
4.	
5.	
6.	
7.	
8.	
9.	
10.	

Answer Sheet

Television Sitcoms
2 Rolls

Name_____

1.	
2.	
3.	
4.	
5.	
6.	
7.	
8.	
9.	
10.	

After you have filled out the sheet, fold your column underneath along the dashed line so the next restroom user won't see your answers. *The first player uses the far right column.*

Notes: *Notes:*   *Notes:*

Television Sitcoms

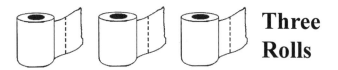

Three Rolls

Flip to pg. 70 for answers

1. What sitcom of the late 1970s and early 1980s had Mel "kissing grits"?

2. What sitcom had Mr. Furley and The Ropers believing that a male tenant was dating two female roommates?

3. One of the greatest writers and producers in TV history, he produced or wrote *All in Family*, *The Jeffersons*, *Sanford and Son*, *Maude*, and *Good Times*. Name him.

4. What show of the 1980s and early 1990s had the musical hit, *Thank You for Being a Friend*, as its theme song? Well, it was four friends in particular.

5. Who was Carol Burnett saying hello to when she tugged on her ear at the end of each show?

6. How many kids were offspring of Cliff Huxtable on *The Cosby Show*? As if being a doctor and a lawyer wasn't enough work for the nice couple.

7. What actress did Kirstie Alley replace on *Cheers*?

8. Who did Bob Newhart wake up next to in the final scene of *Newhart*?

9. Where was the secret passageway that allowed Webster to sneak through the house?

10. What late 1980s hit featured a girl who was half alien, and could freeze time by touching her index fingers together? She would talk to her dad every so often from a glowing diamond-shaped orb.

Answer Sheet

Television Sitcoms
3 Rolls

Name_____

1.
2.
3.
4.
5.
6.
7.
8.
9.
10.

Answer Sheet

Television Sitcoms
3 Rolls

Name_____

1.
2.
3.
4.
5.
6.
7.
8.
9.
10.

Answer Sheet

Television Sitcoms
3 Rolls

Name_____

1.
2.
3.
4.
5.
6.
7.
8.
9.
10.

After you have filled out the sheet, fold your column underneath along the dashed line so the next restroom user won't see your answers. *The first player uses the far right column.*

Notes:

Notes:

Notes:

Fads

 **One Roll**

Flip to pg. 71 for answers

1. What was the most popular dance of the Roaring 20s? It was named for a city in South Carolina.

2. In its first four months of sales in 1958, what plastic exercise ring was sold over 25 million times?

3. What dance movement of the 1970s would not be complete without a large mirrored spinning ball atop the center of the dance floor?

4. What type of pants popular in the 1960s and 1970s gradually widen from the knee to the ankle?

5. What dance craze of the mid-1990s involved arms out, turn hand, hand to shoulder, hand to head, hands to hips, hands to butt, shake, jump?

6. Glowing liquid and wax concoctions have made a comeback. Do you know what they are called, or are you still living in the dark?

7. This famous toy was laughing all the way to the bank considering that some parents were willing to pay over $1,000 for it in the 1996 holiday season.

8. What cuddly product of the late 1990s and beyond would every so often "retire" one of its members? When this happened, its value would go through the roof...unfortunately, it would also attract counterfeiters.

9. Once known as the "Lazy Spring," this object that can walk down stairs is more commonly known as this.

10. A popular fad of the late 1950s has come back stronger than ever in recent years. Just ask those who play this "ultimate" sport.

Answer Sheet

Fads
1 Roll

Name_____

1.

2.

3.

4.

5.

6.

7.

8.

9.

10.

Answer Sheet

Fads
1 Roll

Name_____

1.

2.

3.

4.

5.

6.

7.

8.

9.

10.

Answer Sheet

Fads
1 Roll

Name_____

1.

2.

3.

4.

5.

6.

7.

8.

9.

10.

After you have filled out the sheet, fold your column underneath along the dashed line so the next restroom user won't see your answers. *The first player uses the far right column.*

Notes:

Notes:

Notes:

Fads

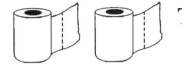

Two Rolls

Flip to pg. 72 for answers

1. Just before 2000, people started saying "Was-sup!" What product was that popular commercial quotation referring to?

2. What collector's item/game pieces of the early 1990s were circular, made of cardboard, and had images of whatever interested you on the front?

3. What item has recently been taken out of packs of baseball cards because it might damage the merchandise? Or, it just might go stale.

4. What non-living companion of the 1970s came in a box with breathable holes and straw on the bottom? Neither was necessary.

5. "The Hollywood Diet" instructed people to eat what fruit in place of meal components?

6. Just before the spread of cellphones, what did people use to alert friends to call them?

7. What was the three character abbreviation for "Oh no! We are turning the new millennium. Computers won't know what year it is!"

8. What winter gloves, short-lived in the 1980s, changed color when you went out into the cold?

9. A popular way to play music during the late 1960s and 1970s, what contemporary of the cassette tape died out by the early 1980s?

10. What fad of the 1920s and 1930s involved couples trying to stay on their feet for the longest time possible? Sometimes they would collapse or simply fall asleep in each other's arms.

Answer Sheet

Fads
2 Rolls

Name_____

Answer Sheet

Fads
2 Rolls

Name_____

Answer Sheet

Fads
2 Rolls

Name_____

1.	1.	1.
2.	2.	2.
3.	3.	3.
4.	4.	4.
5.	5.	5.
6.	6.	6.
7.	7.	7.
8.	8.	8.
9.	9.	9.
10.	10.	10.

After you have filled out the sheet, fold your column underneath along the dashed line so the next restroom user won't see your answers. *The first player uses the far right column.*

Notes:

Notes:

Notes:

Fads

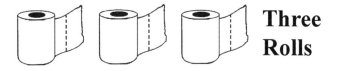

Three Rolls

Flip to pg. 73 for answers

1. What trading cards poked fun at one of the most popular holiday dolls of the 1980s?

2. What fad among children of the late 1980s was wrist jewelry that could be flattened?

3. How many squares are on a Rubik's Cube?

4. What dolls look like they stuck their fingers into an electrical socket? People loved to collect them wearing different outfits.

5. Alvin "Shipwreck" Kelly was the most famous man to ever do what on top of a building?

6. What type of accessory was popularized by Dwayne Wayne on the sitcom *A Different World*?

7. *Dick Tracy* wore what type of clothing that was popularized in the 1930s and 1940s? It had baggy pants, large lapels, sometimes bright colors, high waist, tight cuffs, and a long coat.

8. What toy involved rubbing an image with a pencil, then pulling a plastic sheet to permanently place it?

9. What piece of jewelry popular in the 1970s was said to alter its color when the emotional state of the person wearing it changed?

10. What was the female version of the 1980s doll My Buddy called?

Answer Sheet
Fads
3 Rolls

Name_____

Answer Sheet
Fads
3 Rolls

Name_____

Answer Sheet
Fads
3 Rolls

Name_____

1.	1.	1.
2.	2.	2.
3.	3.	3.
4.	4.	4.
5.	5.	5.
6.	6.	6.
7.	7.	7.
8.	8.	8.
9.	9.	9.
10.	10.	10.

After you have filled out the sheet, fold your column underneath along the dashed line so the next restroom user won't see your answers. *The first player uses the far right column.*

Notes: *Notes:*   *Notes:*

Radio

 **One Roll**

Flip to pg. 74 for answers

1. Who is the self-proclaimed, "King of All Media?"

2. What US government agency was set up in 1934 to regulate radio? Today, it does the same for television.

3. What legendary voice hosted *American Top 40* from "coast to coast" for over 20 years? He was also the voice behind Shaggy on *Scooby Doo*.

4. Though he rocked the microphone counting down top hits, this DJ was better known for how he rocked New Year's Eve.

5. Name the show or personality that made New Jersey think that the Martians were attacking on Halloween Eve, 1938?

6. What 1987 movie put Robin Williams as a wake-up DJ in Saigon?

7. What legendary comedian established "the seven dirty words" you can't say on the air? We won't ask you to name them ... unless you really want to.

8. Which conservative talk show host became a best-selling author with his *The Way Things Ought to Be*, and *See, I Told You So*?

9. Before anyone ever saw Tonto, they heard him on what famous radio show of the 1930s and beyond?

10. What were the first two companies to commercially offer satellite radio?

Answer Sheet

Radio
1 Roll

Name_____

Answer Sheet

Radio
1 Roll

Name_____

Answer Sheet

Radio
1 Roll

Name_____

1.	1.	1.
2.	2.	2.
3.	3.	3.
4.	4.	4.
5.	5.	5.
6.	6.	6.
7.	7.	7.
8.	8.	8.
9.	9.	9.
10.	10.	10.

After you have filled out the sheet, fold your column underneath along the dashed line so the next restroom user won't see your answers. *The first player uses the far right column.*

Notes: *Notes:*   *Notes:*

Radio

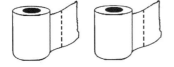 **Two Rolls**

Flip to pg. 75 for answers

1. What DJ in a cowboy hat was broadcast by MSNBC in its first year?

2. What national radio entity does not have commercials? Rather it has underwritings, which are short factual statements without prices or bias.

3. Known as "The Moondog," and creator of the term "Rock and Roll," what pioneer record-spinner pleaded guilty for payola in 1962?

4. A sometimes controversial radio talk show host, she was the first woman to win the Marconi Award for Personality of the Year in 1997. She penned *Ten Stupid Things Women Do to Mess Up Their Lives*.

5. Name one of the two horses that raced on November 1, 1938 in the "Match of the Century," where about 40 million listeners tuned in.

6. What call letters were in the title of a popular radio-themed TV sitcom based in Cincinnati?

7. The first official radio station in American history was KDKA. Today, it's one of the few radio stations with a "K" east of the Mississippi River. Where is KDKA?

8. What present doctor was giving out medical advice on *Lovelines* in 1984 during his fourth year of medical school?

9. Who reported live from the blitz in London during World War II, and was also the commentator who criticized Senator Joseph McCarthy?

10. What hit by The Buggles was fittingly the first music video ever played on MTV?

Answer Sheet   Answer Sheet   Answer Sheet

Radio   **Radio**   **Radio**
2 Rolls   **2 Rolls**   **2 Rolls**

Name_____   Name_____   Name_____

1.	1.	1.
2.	2.	2.
3.	3.	3.
4.	4.	4.
5.	5.	5.
6.	6.	6.
7.	7.	7.
8.	8.	8.
9.	9.	9.
10.	10.	10.

After you have filled out the sheet, fold your column underneath along the dashed line so the next restroom user won't see your answers. ***The first player uses the far right column.***

Notes: *Notes:*   *Notes:*

Radio

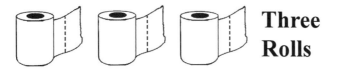

Three Rolls

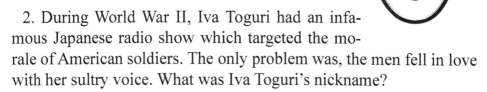

Flip to pg. 76 for answers

1. Name one of the voices behind *Amos 'n' Andy*.

2. During World War II, Iva Toguri had an infamous Japanese radio show which targeted the morale of American soldiers. The only problem was, the men fell in love with her sultry voice. What was Iva Toguri's nickname?

3. What was the country's first all sports radio station? It debuted in New York a year after the Mets won the World Series.

4. Which comedian's variety show featured appearances by Mel Blanc, the voice of Bugs Bunny? *You should think it over*.

5. One of the most popular radio stunts done by this comedy duo was giving away "100 Grand," that turned out to be a 100 Grand Bar.

6. *How 'Bout That!* Inducted into the National Radio Hall of Fame in 1988, he was the voice of the New York Yankees.

7. Tom and Ray Magliozzi are just two normal mechanics. Put a microphone behind them, and you have what famous public radio show?

8. What 1988 Oliver Stone film featured a controversial Dallas DJ who was gunned down by a neo-Nazi? It was based on a true story.

9. Have you ever wondered what AM and FM stand for? OK, just tell us one of them.

10. What famous former MTV Video-DJ has helped to revolutionize internet radio with the podcast? Some have referred to him as "The Podfather."

Answer Sheet Answer Sheet Answer Sheet

Radio
3 Rolls

Radio
3 Rolls

Radio
3 Rolls

Name_____ Name_____ Name_____

1.	1.	1.
2.	2.	2.
3.	3.	3.
4.	4.	4.
5.	5.	5.
6.	6.	6.
7.	7.	7.
8.	8.	8.
9.	9.	9.
10.	10.	10.

After you have filled out the sheet, fold your column underneath along the dashed line so the next restroom user won't see your answers. *The first player uses the far right column.*

Notes: *Notes:*   *Notes:*

Famous People

 ## One Roll

Flip to pg. 77 for answers

1. Who is Judy Garland's famous daughter?

2. What Oscar-winning actor started his own food company where profits go to charity? You've seen his face on bottles and jars.

3. Which celebrity is the president of Harpo Productions, Inc.? If you don't know, then read this question backwards.

4. What comedic actor and writer never curbed any of his enthusiasm about being the voice of George Steinbrenner on *Seinfeld*?

5. What legendary singer admitted that she would rather have been an actress? She got her chance nonetheless, and even today a new generation knows her as Mrs. Focker.

6. More than a *contender*, this *Godfather* of acting was in almost 50 movies.

7. Before he became a worldwide movie star, this celebrity was Dr. Ross on *ER*.

8. Name one of the two actors who played Bill and Ted in the movie, *Bill and Ted's Excellent Adventure*.

9. Master of the song parody, what polka-loving musician also starred in his own movie, *UHF*?

10. Many celebrities have played the President of the United States. But who was the only Hollywood actor to do it in real life?

Answer Sheet | Answer Sheet | Answer Sheet

**Famous People
1 Roll**

**Famous People
1 Roll**

**Famous People
1 Roll**

Name_____   Name_____   Name_____

1.	1.	1.
2.	2.	2.
3.	3.	3.
4.	4.	4.
5.	5.	5.
6.	6.	6.
7.	7.	7.
8.	8.	8.
9.	9.	9.
10.	10.	10.

After you have filled out the sheet, fold your column underneath along the dashed line so the next restroom user won't see your answers. *The first player uses the far right column.*

Notes: *Notes:*   *Notes:*

Famous People

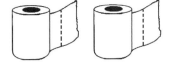

Two Rolls

Flip to pg. 78 for answers

1. What CBS News anchor was "The Most Trusted Man in America?"

2. A comedy tag team partner of Dean Martin, this man is known by new generations as the chairman of the Muscular Dystrophy Association.

3. Who has the most Oscars for Best Actress? She won her first and last almost 50 years apart!

4. Who took advantage of his own toothbrush mustache to play Hitler in the 1940 movie, *The Great Dictator*?

5. There are four Baldwin brothers. Name three of them.

6. In the early years of rap, what famous actor debuted *Parents Just Don't Understand* with his childhood friend DJ Jazzy Jeff? They won the first ever Grammy for Best Rap Performance in 1989.

7. What was Marilyn Monroe's name at birth?

8. A year before this actor played the lead opposite Daryl Hannah in *Splash*, he was Uncle Ned, a visiting alcoholic on *Family Ties*.

9. Name one of the two actors nominated for an Oscar in every decade from the 1960s to the 2000s.

10. What famous Swedish actress who began working in the silent film era was really named Greta Lovisa Gustafsson?

Answer Sheet Answer Sheet Answer Sheet

Famous People
2 Rolls

Famous People
2 Rolls

Famous People
2 Rolls

Name_____ Name_____ Name_____

1.	1.	1.
2.	2.	2.
3.	3.	3.
4.	4.	4.
5.	5.	5.
6.	6.	6.
7.	7.	7.
8.	8.	8.
9.	9.	9.
10.	10.	10.

After you have filled out the sheet, fold your column underneath along the dashed line so the next restroom user won't see your answers. *The first player uses the far right column.*

Notes: *Notes:*   *Notes:*

Famous People

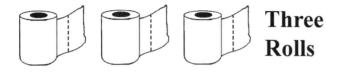

Three Rolls

Flip to pg. 79 for answers

1. How many husbands did Elizabeth Taylor have?

2. One of this TV personality's first jobs was talking to customers behind the candy counter at Macy's. Food and talking is really her thing.

3. Did you know that Jennifer Aniston's father is famous? John Aniston has been acting since the 1960s. For decades he's been Victor Kiriakis on what soap opera?

4. What famous actor who played *Kojak* shaved his head before it was cool to do so?

5. One of the first heartthrobs in entertainment history, what early film actor's most famous role was *The Shiek*? His death at the age of 31 created panic and hysteria among female fans.

6. Twelve people on Earth have won each of the major awards in Entertainment: an Emmy, Grammy, Oscar, and Tony. Can you name four of the twelve? *Note*: Not all are actors.

7. What movie was Jim Carrey's first leading role in which he was seduced by a vampire played by Lauren Hutton?

8. Who were the three comedians that hosted the first HBO *Comic Relief*?

9. What famous late night talk show host started as a weatherman predicting hail "the size of canned hams"?

10. What now-divorced celebrity couple had an on-screen romance on the set of *Days of Thunder*?

Answer Sheet | Answer Sheet | Answer Sheet

Famous People
3 Rolls

Famous People
3 Rolls

Famous People
3 Rolls

Name_____ Name_____ Name_____

1.	1.	1.
2.	2.	2.
3.	3.	3.
4.	4.	4.
5.	5.	5.
6.	6.	6.
7.	7.	7.
8.	8.	8.
9.	9.	9.
10.	10.	10.

After you have filled out the sheet, fold your column underneath along the dashed line so the next restroom user won't see your answers. *The first player uses the far right column.*

Notes: *Notes:*   *Notes:*

Movies

 ## One Roll

Flip to pg. 80 for answers

1. What was the name of the pirate in *The Goonies*?

2. What 1976 movie was the first sports film to win the Oscar for Best Picture?

3. What 1979 Vietnam War masterpiece of Francis Ford Coppola had so many famous actors in it, that Harrison Ford only had a small part? Marlon Brando, Martin Sheen, Robert Duvall, Laurence Fishburne, and Dennis Hopper were also in the cast.

4. Name the cult musical or film of the mid-1970s that featured *The Time Warp Dance*.

5. Which classic 1939 movie had a nasty rumor that one of its actors committed suicide while on camera?

6. In what movie series did a time machine run on 1.21 Gigawatts?

7. In what movie did Marlon Brando give the Contender Speech?

8. What famous boxer punches Alan in the face in *The Hangover*?

9. In what movie did Leslie Nielsen voice displeasure about being called "Shirley?"

10. What did Superman hope to accomplish by repeatedly flying around the world at light speed?

Answer Sheet | Answer Sheet | Answer Sheet

Movies
1 Roll

Movies
1 Roll

Movies
1 Roll

Name_____ | Name_____ | Name_____

1.	1.	1.
2.	2.	2.
3.	3.	3.
4.	4.	4.
5.	5.	5.
6.	6.	6.
7.	7.	7.
8.	8.	8.
9.	9.	9.
10.	10.	10.

After you have filled out the sheet, fold your column underneath along the dashed line so the next restroom user won't see your answers. *The first player uses the far right column.*

Notes: | *Notes:* | *Notes:*

Movies

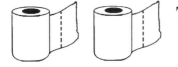

Two Rolls

Flip to pg. 81 for answers

1. What two polar opposites were *Twins* in a 1988 comedy?

2. Which American horror series has the most sequels?

3. What three presidents did Forrest Gump personally meet at the White House?

4. What movie begins with Pumpkin and Honey Bunny holding up a diner?

5. In what movie did Rob Reiner's mother tell a waitress that she wanted to order what Meg Ryan was having?

6. In 1992, a couple of kids were in trouble down South. Joe Pesci played what relative and attorney that set them free?

7. In the *Austin Powers* series, what is the name of Dr. Evil's son played by Seth Green?

8. What was used as a special effect for blood in the shower scene of Alfred Hitchcock's *Psycho*?

9. What celebrity game show host does Adam Sandler trade punches with in *Happy Gilmore*?

10. What gigantic edible creature wreaked havoc on New York City at the end of the original *Ghostbusters*?

Answer Sheet　Answer Sheet　Answer Sheet

Movies
2 Rolls

Movies
2 Rolls

Movies
2 Rolls

Name_____　Name_____　Name_____

1.	1.	1.
2.	2.	2.
3.	3.	3.
4.	4.	4.
5.	5.	5.
6.	6.	6.
7.	7.	7.
8.	8.	8.
9.	9.	9.
10.	10.	10.

After you have filled out the sheet, fold your column underneath along the dashed line so the next restroom user won't see your answers. *The first player uses the far right column.*

Notes:　*Notes:*　*Notes:*

Movies

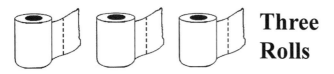

Three Rolls

Flip to pg. 82 for answers

1. What was Mickey Mouse's first animated short?

2. Of the following four lengthy films, which one's original release was the longest? *Gone with the Wind* (1939), *The Ten Commandments* (1956), *Ben Hur* (1959), *Titanic* (1997).

3. Who directed *Superman*, *Lethal Weapon*, and *The Goonies*?

4. At the Oscars, "Best Picture" used to be referred to as "Outstanding Picture." What film won the first Oscar for this category? It was a silent film about a World War I fighter pilot.

5. Martin Scorsese's *Goodfellas* was based on the life story of what former mobster? He has since come out of hiding, and has even filmed a TV episode of *Locked Up Abroad*. He's also been known to call into the *Howard Stern Show*.

6. In Rock Ridge from *Blazing Saddles*, what was the last name of everyone in the town?

7. In what fictional seaside community did *Jaws* take place?

8. Risking a hefty fine, what producer of *Gone with the Wind* chose to keep the word "damn" in the production?

9. What team did Paul Newman's character play and coach for in *Slap Shot*?

10. Who was the famous voice behind Darth Vader in the original *Star Wars* trilogy?

Answer Sheet

Movies
3 Rolls

Answer Sheet

Movies
3 Rolls

Answer Sheet

Movies
3 Rolls

Name_____   Name_____   Name_____

1.	1.	1.
2.	2.	2.
3.	3.	3.
4.	4.	4.
5.	5.	5.
6.	6.	6.
7.	7.	7.
8.	8.	8.
9.	9.	9.
10.	10.	10.

After you have filled out the sheet, fold your column underneath along the dashed line so the next restroom user won't see your answers. *The first player uses the far right column.*

Notes: *Notes:*   *Notes:*

Food & Drink

 ## One Roll

Flip to pg. 83 for answers

1. What company sponsors the July 4th Hot Dog Eating Contest at Coney Island?

2. In the early years of H. J. Heinz, how many product varieties did they offer?

3. What celebrity's hair accidentally caught on fire while filming a 1984 Pepsi commercial?

4. What is the name of the comic character inside every piece of Bazooka gum?

5. What worldwide coffee company based out of Seattle is named for a character from *Moby Dick*?

6. What type of Oreo introduced in 1975 has twice as much filling inside compared to the original?

7. Who are the three little mascots in a bowl of Rice Krispies?

8. What food mascot has an eyeglass, top hat, and cane?

9. What line of foods was started by Italian immigrant Ettore Boiardi?

10. What famous chain of eateries was created by Glen *Bell*?

Answer Sheet

Food & Drink
1 Roll

Name_____

Answer Sheet

Food & Drink
1 Roll

Name_____

Answer Sheet

Food & Drink
1 Roll

Name_____

1.	1.	1.
2.	2.	2.
3.	3.	3.
4.	4.	4.
5.	5.	5.
6.	6.	6.
7.	7.	7.
8.	8.	8.
9.	9.	9.
10.	10.	10.

After you have filled out the sheet, fold your column underneath along the dashed line so the next restroom user won't see your answers. ***The first player uses the far right column.***

Notes: *Notes:*   *Notes:*

Food & Drink

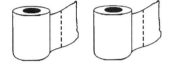

Two Rolls

Flip to pg. 84 for answers

1. What color of M&M's disappeared from 1976-1987?

2. What chain of restaurants originated the square hamburger as a means to fit more on the grill?

3. In what city would one find pictures of Colonel Sanders draped on the walls of the buildings, and a wax figure of him greeting people at a welcome center?

4. What word was added to Coca-Cola after the company scrapped the New Coke recipe in 1985?

5. What Boston beer company is named for a man who is more remembered for tea?

6. Name the four candies inside a Hershey's Miniatures Classic Assortment.

7. What company claims to answer to an "authority" more elevated than the Federal Government?

8. In 1948, Chocolate Mint became what numbered flavor at Baskin-Robbins?

9. What beverage is named for the college football team it was tested on?

10. How many holes are in the bottom of a traditional Hostess Twinkie?

Answer Sheet

Food & Drink
2 Rolls

Name_____

Answer Sheet

Food & Drink
2 Rolls

Name_____

Answer Sheet

Food & Drink
2 Rolls

Name_____

1.	1.	1.
2.	2.	2.
3.	3.	3.
4.	4.	4.
5.	5.	5.
6.	6.	6.
7.	7.	7.
8.	8.	8.
9.	9.	9.
10.	10.	10.

After you have filled out the sheet, fold your column underneath along the dashed line so the next restroom user won't see your answers. *The first player uses the far right column.*

Notes: *Notes:*   *Notes:*

Food & Drink

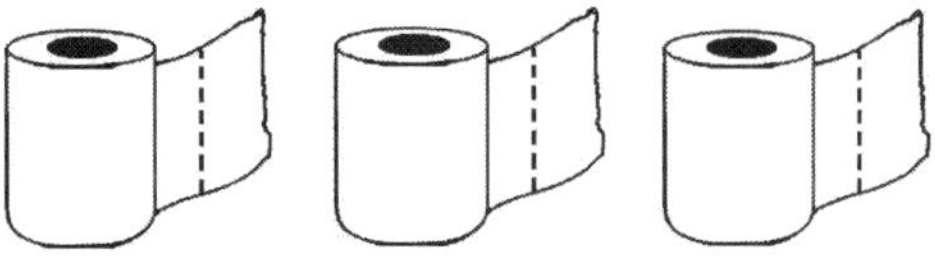

Three Rolls

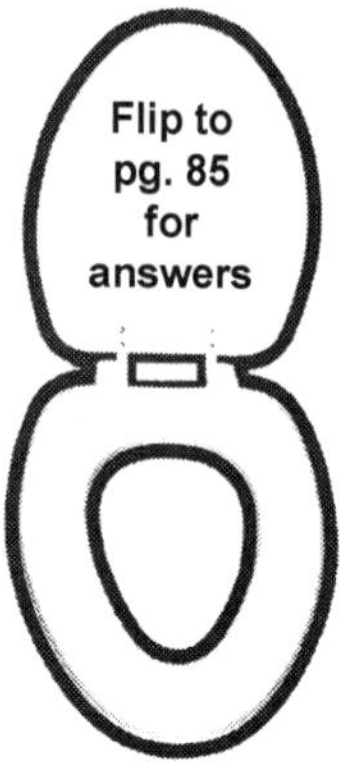
Flip to
pg. 85
for
answers

1. What famous celebrity was the first to play Ronald McDonald?

2. What is the name of Sailor Jack's dog on a box of Cracker Jack?

3. Who is the Baby Ruth candy bar named for?

4. Put the following hamburger establishments in order of when they first opened: Burger King, McDonald's, Wendy's, White Castle.

5. Besides Count Chocula, name one other Monster Cereal put out by General Mills.

6. What canned American classic has its own museum in Austin, Minnesota?

7. What nationwide corn chip recipe was purchased for $100 by Elmer Doolin in San Antonio, Texas in 1932?

8. What chain of restaurants was started by a 17 year-old looking to pay for medical school?

9. What product's logo contains blue, red, and yellow circles that are supposed to represent balloons?

10. What company that used to be called Florida Foods, and Vacuum Foods Corporation, shipped the first concentrated orange juice product in 1945?

Answer Sheet

Food & Drink
3 Rolls

Name_____

Answer Sheet

Food & Drink
3 Rolls

Name_____

Answer Sheet

Food & Drink
3 Rolls

Name_____

1.	1.	1.
2.	2.	2.
3.	3.	3.
4.	4.	4.
5.	5.	5.
6.	6.	6.
7.	7.	7.
8.	8.	8.
9.	9.	9.
10.	10.	10.

After you have filled out the sheet, fold your column underneath along the dashed line so the next restroom user won't see your answers. *The first player uses the far right column.*

Notes: *Notes:* *Notes:*

Music

 ## One Roll

Flip to pg. 86 for answers

1. What future wife of Billy Joel played the lead role in the *Uptown Girl* video?

2. What famous singer was born in New York, but *left his heart* on the West Coast? Fittingly, he would sing a duet with Frank Sinatra for *New York, New York* in 1993.

3. What album has sold the most copies worldwide?

4. What was the name of the Guns N' Roses debut album which included *Welcome to the Jungle* and *Sweet Child o' Mine*?

5. In what city is the Rock and Roll Hall of Fame located? One might say that this city rocks.

6. Who electrified the Woodstock audience in 1969 with his rendition of *The Star Spangled Banner*?

7. What legendary "man in black" was reintroduced to a new generation of fans when he did a remake of *Nine Inch Nails'* song *Hurt* in 2002?

8. What musical duo had their Grammy revoked in 1990 for lipsynching *Blame it on the Rain*?

9. What Irish-born singer is Paul David Hewson better known as?

10. What pop duet shared the Number One single *I Got You Babe* in 1965? They shared more than that in real life.

Answer Sheet

Music
1 Roll

Name_____

Answer Sheet

Music
1 Roll

Name_____

Answer Sheet

Music
1 Roll

Name_____

1.	1.	1.
2.	2.	2.
3.	3.	3.
4.	4.	4.
5.	5.	5.
6.	6.	6.
7.	7.	7.
8.	8.	8.
9.	9.	9.
10.	10.	10.

After you have filled out the sheet, fold your column underneath along the dashed line so the next restroom user won't see your answers. *The first player uses the far right column.*

Notes:

Notes:

Notes:

Music

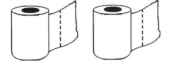

Two Rolls

Flip to pg. 87 for answers

1. What event happened on the day that Don McLean considered music to die?

2. What famous musician wrote the jingle for State Farm Insurance, and the Band-Aid one that got stuck in your head? I guess he didn't just *write the songs*.

3. What band asked people to *Whip It*?

4. Eminem is also referred to as this alter ego.

5. Who sang an electronic duet of *Unforgettable* with her deceased father in 1991?

6. What band was formed by Nirvana drummer Dave Grohl in 1994? It is named for odd UFO orbs of light that dotted the skies of Europe during World War II.

7. What two members of Led Zeppelin wrote *Stairway to Heaven*?

8. What Queen of Soul wore a hat with a tremendous bow on it as she sang at President Barack Obama's inauguration in 2009?

9. Jim Morrison, lead singer of The Doors, is buried in what city?

10. What was the first Madonna single to hit Number One on the *Billboard* Hot 100 chart?

Answer Sheet | Answer Sheet | Answer Sheet

Music
2 Rolls

Music
2 Rolls

Music
2 Rolls

Name_____ Name_____ Name_____

1.	1.	1.
2.	2.	2.
3.	3.	3.
4.	4.	4.
5.	5.	5.
6.	6.	6.
7.	7.	7.
8.	8.	8.
9.	9.	9.
10.	10.	10.

After you have filled out the sheet, fold your column underneath along the dashed line so the next restroom user won't see your answers. ***The first player uses the far right column.***

Notes: | *Notes:* | *Notes:*

Music

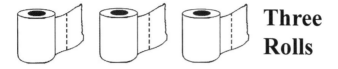

Three Rolls

Flip to pg. 88 for answers

1. What was the first single that went to Number One for Elvis Presley?

2. What name is on Jay-Z's birth certificate?

3. Bob Dylan's son, Jakob, is the lead singer of what band that won the Best Rock Song Grammy for *One Headlight* in 1998?

4. Saul Hudson, or Slash, co-founded what band after the break up of Guns N' Roses?

5. What rock band's drummer played with one arm after losing the other one in a car accident?

6. What folk contemporary of Bob Dylan and Joan Baez was famous for *I Ain't Marchin' Anymore*, *There But for Fortune*, and *Love Me, I'm a Liberal*?

7. What famous rubberband-wearing wrestler played the role of Cyndi Lauper's father in the video of *Girls Just Want to Have Fun*?

8. For charity, David Bowie and Mick Jagger remade *Dancing in the Street* in 1985. Who originally recorded this Motown classic in 1964?

9. What short-lived band comprised of legends George Harrison, Bob Dylan, Roy Orbison, Tom Petty, and Jeff Lynne had their biggest hit in 1988 with *Handle with Care*?

10. What 14 year-old country star became the youngest to win a Grammy in 1996 after releasing her album, *Blue*?

Answer Sheet

Music
3 Rolls

Name_____

Answer Sheet

Music
3 Rolls

Name_____

Answer Sheet

Music
3 Rolls

Name_____

1.	1.	1.
2.	2.	2.
3.	3.	3.
4.	4.	4.
5.	5.	5.
6.	6.	6.
7.	7.	7.
8.	8.	8.
9.	9.	9.
10.	10.	10.

After you have filled out the sheet, fold your column underneath along the dashed line so the next restroom user won't see your answers. ***The first player uses the far right column.***

Notes:

Notes:

Notes:

Games & Video Games

 One Roll

Flip to pg. 89 for answers

1. What two properties make up the most expensive set in Monopoly?

2. What game that comes with Microsoft Windows involves attempting to find bombs? Usually, you can find out how many are nearby, other times, you better have good luck!

3. What two-dimensional form of tennis was one of the first arcade games of all time?

4. In Hearts, what card penalizes you 13 points? Unless of course, you are shooting the moon.

5. Name the fighting game involving Sub Zero, Scorpion, and a bunch of other warriors who can do gruesome moves when the screen says, "Finish Him." An entire generation of kids would scream the title out of their windows.

6. How many points is a "Z" worth in Scrabble?

7. Which game that involves stacking 54 wooden blocks could end in a big mess if you pulled out the wrong one from the bottom?

8. What fruit is on the first board of *Pac-Man* and *Ms. Pac-Man*?

9. What board game that involves physical dexterity has you removing organs from a body? You better not hit the metal edge with those tweezers!

10. What shape-flipping video game was created in the Soviet Union?

Answer Sheet

Games & Video Games
1 Roll

Name_____

Answer Sheet

Games & Video Games
1 Roll

Name_____

Answer Sheet

Games & Video Games
1 Roll

Name_____

1.	1.	1.
2.	2.	2.
3.	3.	3.
4.	4.	4.
5.	5.	5.
6.	6.	6.
7.	7.	7.
8.	8.	8.
9.	9.	9.
10.	10.	10.

After you have filled out the sheet, fold your column underneath along the dashed line so the next restroom user won't see your answers. *The first player uses the far right column.*

Notes: *Notes:*   *Notes:*

Games & Video Games

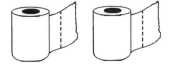

Two Rolls

Flip to pg. 90 for answers

1. What children's board game contains four similar mammals trying to eat marbles?

2. What popular World War II series of video games, now played mostly on consoles, was originally produced by Activision for the PC in 2003?

3. B1...Hit. B2...Hit. B3...Hit. B4...Hit. Something just sank in what game?

4. What party game makes you describe a word, without saying five other words, or the word itself? Don't say the wrong thing, or you might get the buzzer!

5. In the *Super Mario Bros.* series, what type of object makes Mario get bigger?

6. What popular game includes the cards of Skip, Draw 2, Wild, and Reverse?

7. Who is the first opponent on *Punch Out!!*, or *Mike Tyson's Punch Out!!*? It's almost impossible to lose to him!

8. How many squares on a traditional chess or checkerboard?

9. Abbreviated WoW, which online multi-player has you controlling an "avatar," or "toon?"

10. What two-on-two basketball video game involves players heating up and then catching on fire?

Answer Sheet

Games & Video Games
2 Rolls

Name_____

Answer Sheet

Games & Video Games
2 Rolls

Name_____

Answer Sheet

Games & Video Games
2 Rolls

Name_____

1.	1.	1.
2.	2.	2.
3.	3.	3.
4.	4.	4.
5.	5.	5.
6.	6.	6.
7.	7.	7.
8.	8.	8.
9.	9.	9.
10.	10.	10.

After you have filled out the sheet, fold your column underneath along the dashed line so the next restroom user won't see your answers. *The first player uses the far right column.*

Notes: *Notes:*   *Notes:*

Games & Video Games

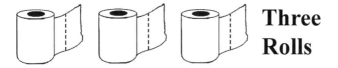

Three Rolls

Flip to pg. 91 for answers

1. What strategic card game played with a 48-card deck looks to get melds and tricks?

2. What was the original name of *Madden NFL*?

3. Which board game similar to Parcheesi attempts to get four colored pegs from "Start" to "Home"?

4. What Nintendo Entertainment System hockey game penalized the team that lost the fights? When you turned the game on, it would say the title in muffled speech.

5. Name four of the six suspects in Clue.

6. What Atari game used a paddle to keep bombs from hitting the ground?

7. Which popular board game involves shaking 16 cubed dice with letters on them, and then making as many words as possible out of the letters displayed?

8. What was Sega's first hand-held portable color video game system that rivaled Game Boy?

9. How many colors can be spun for in a game of Twister?

10. In what original video game classic does Link have to defeat Ganon?

Answer Sheet

Games & Video Games
3 Rolls

Name_____

Answer Sheet

Games & Video Games
3 Rolls

Name_____

Answer Sheet

Games & Video Games
3 Rolls

Name_____

1.	1.	1.
2.	2.	2.
3.	3.	3.
4.	4.	4.
5.	5.	5.
6.	6.	6.
7.	7.	7.
8.	8.	8.
9.	9.	9.
10.	10.	10.

After you have filled out the sheet, fold your column underneath along the dashed line so the next restroom user won't see your answers. *The first player uses the far right column.*

Notes:

Notes:

Notes:

Game Shows

 ## One Roll

Flip to pg. 92 for answers

1. What has been the longest running game show in TV history?

2. What game show gives you three lifelines to win a million dollars?

3. What former talk show host was the brains behind *Jeopardy!* and *Wheel of Fortune*?

4. On *Press Your Luck*, what was the name of the red creature that took away all of the contestant's money?

5. During the closing credits of which show would the host offer people in the audience money if they could produce a particular item?

6. Whose popularity as a player on *Match Game* propelled him to become the "kissing host" of *Family Feud*?

7. What game show has 11 year-olds schooling adults?

8. Who is the winningest game show contestant of all time?

9. Whose money were contestants trying to win on a game show hosted by Jimmy Kimmel?

10. On what show can you only be a contestant if you have been married for less than two years?

Answer Sheet

Game Shows
1 Roll

Name_____

1.
2.
3.
4.
5.
6.
7.
8.
9.
10.

Answer Sheet

Game Shows
1 Roll

Name_____

1.
2.
3.
4.
5.
6.
7.
8.
9.
10.

Answer Sheet

Game Shows
1 Roll

Name_____

1.
2.
3.
4.
5.
6.
7.
8.
9.
10.

After you have filled out the sheet, fold your column underneath along the dashed line so the next restroom user won't see your answers. ***The first player uses the far right column.***

Notes:

Notes:

Notes:

Game Shows

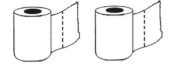

Two Rolls

Flip to pg. 93 for answers

1. Who was the host of *Jeopardy!* before Alex Trebek?

2. On what show could a celebrity judge end an act by hitting a Chinese piece of bronze? Judges would sometimes fight over who would do it first!

3. How many spaces are on the wheel spun by contestants on *The Price is Right*?

4. Who co-hosted the first *American Idol* season alongside Ryan Seacrest?

5. What show saw Alan Freed, Rosa Parks, Larry King, and many others defending their identities against two imposters?

6. What *The Golden Girls* actress made dozens of appearances on *Password*, *$25,000 Pyramid*, and *Match Game*? She was respected by many to be one of the best partners on each show.

7. Have you ever taken a taxi in New York City? You better be careful, or you might wind up on this cable game show.

8. On what game show without celebrity squares, would players place X's and O's after answering questions correctly?

9. Vicky Lawrence hosted a daytime show in the late 1980s based on Pictionary. What was it called?

10. Six letters that were historically chosen almost all of the time are now provided to contestants in the final round of Wheel of Fortune. Name four of them.

Answer Sheet | Answer Sheet | Answer Sheet

Game Shows
2 Rolls

Name_____ Name_____ Name_____

1.	1.	1.
2.	2.	2.
3.	3.	3.
4.	4.	4.
5.	5.	5.
6.	6.	6.
7.	7.	7.
8.	8.	8.
9.	9.	9.
10.	10.	10.

After you have filled out the sheet, fold your column underneath along the dashed line so the next restroom user won't see your answers. *The first player uses the far right column.*

Notes: | *Notes:* | *Notes:*

Game Shows

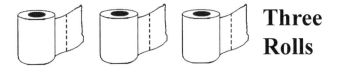

Three Rolls

Flip to pg. 94 for answers

1. Before she turned letters, where did America discover Vanna White as a contestant?

2. In the late 1980s, what frequent center square on *Hollywood Squares* was so popular he sometimes hosted the show? However his witty lines were occasionally a tad "close for comfort."

3. In the Bonus Round of the *$25,000* and *$100,000 Pyramid*, how much money was the box on top of the pyramid worth? (Within $50)

4. What was the name of the big slippery slide that a contestant had to run up in the *Double Dare* obstacle course?

5. In the infamous game show scandal of 1956, what contestant on *Twenty-One* was handed victory over Herb Stempel? Stempel answered a question wrong on purpose.

6. What long-time comedic tag team from *Match Game* died months apart in 2007? They sat on the top row middle, and top row right.

7. How many suitcases can a contestant choose from on *Deal or No Deal*?

8. Nicknamed the "Queen of Mean," on what show did British host Anne Robinson say "goodbye," to contestants?

9. Who hosted *Match Game '73*, as well as the subsequent years?

10. Name the game show that offered *Instant Bargains*, where players would use money accumulated during the game to purchase consumer goods. The show was around in parts of the 1960s, 1970s, and 1980s.

Answer Sheet   Answer Sheet   Answer Sheet

Game Shows   **Game Shows**   **Game Shows**
3 Rolls   **3 Rolls**   **3 Rolls**

Name_____   Name_____   Name_____

1.	1.	1.
2.	2.	2.
3.	3.	3.
4.	4.	4.
5.	5.	5.
6.	6.	6.
7.	7.	7.
8.	8.	8.
9.	9.	9.
10.	10.	10.

After you have filled out the sheet, fold your column underneath along the dashed line so the next restroom user won't see your answers. ***The first player uses the far right column.***

Notes: *Notes:*   *Notes:*

Everything & Anything

 One Roll

Flip to pg. 95 for answers

1. What Broadway show turned movie was about a gigantic people-eating plant?

2. What store did Price Club become?

3. What popular word of the 1960s and 1970s meaning cool, was actually first used decades before?

4. What 20th Century device allowed people to develop their film right after taking a picture?

5. What does HBO stand for?

6. On January 22, 1981, which magazine's cover showed a naked John Lennon cuddling with a fully-clothed Yoko Ono?

7. What has recently passed ketchup to become the most popular tomato-based condiment in the United States?

8. Four zoos in the United States permanently have a "giant panda." Can you name the locations of two of these zoos?

9. Who wrote the horror novel, *It*?

10. What theme park in Orlando, Florida recently added an entire section devoted to *Harry Potter*?

Answer Sheet

Everything & Anything
1 Roll

Name_____

Answer Sheet

Everything & Anything
1 Roll

Name_____

Answer Sheet

Everything & Anything
1 Roll

Name_____

1.	1.	1.
2.	2.	2.
3.	3.	3.
4.	4.	4.
5.	5.	5.
6.	6.	6.
7.	7.	7.
8.	8.	8.
9.	9.	9.
10.	10.	10.

After you have filled out the sheet, fold your column underneath along the dashed line so the next restroom user won't see your answers. *The first player uses the far right column.*

Notes: *Notes:*   *Notes:*

Everything & Anything

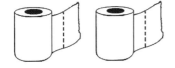

Two Rolls

Flip to pg. 96 for answers

1. What company's character is a bored repairman who never has any work to do?

2. Name three of the four theme parks at Walt Disney World Resort in Orlando, Florida.

3. What type of haircut was popularized by flappers, or women of the 1920s?

4. What company was the first to market frozen meals as TV Dinners in the 1950s?

5. In 1991, what magazine ran a promotion that gave new subscribers a *Sneakerphone*?

6. When *The Phantom of the Opera* became the longest running Broadway show, what did it replace in the record books?

7. As of 2011, what stadium in the United States has the greatest seating capacity?

8. What state did the first Denny's open up in?

9. The Flip Flap Railway opened shortly before 1900 to become America's first looping ride. Where did it open?

10. What commercial character would tell people in supermarkets to refrain from squeezing the Charmin Toilet Paper?

Answer Sheet

Everything & Anything
2 Rolls

Name_____

Answer Sheet

Everything & Anything
2 Rolls

Name_____

Answer Sheet

Everything & Anything
2 Rolls

Name_____

1.	1.	1.
2.	2.	2.
3.	3.	3.
4.	4.	4.
5.	5.	5.
6.	6.	6.
7.	7.	7.
8.	8.	8.
9.	9.	9.
10.	10.	10.

After you have filled out the sheet, fold your column underneath along the dashed line so the next restroom user won't see your answers. ***The first player uses the far right column.***

Notes:

Notes:

Notes:

Everything & Anything

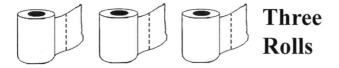

Three Rolls

Flip to pg. 97 for answers

1. What was the name of the bully that tormented Arnold Jackson on *Diff'rent Strokes*?

2. What was the first flavor to be put into chewing gum back in 1884?

3. As of 2011, what park boasts the world's tallest roller coaster?

4. What legendary designer that never went to fashion school opened his first store in 1967? There, he sold wide men's neckties.

5. What converting robot toy was a contemporary of Transformers?

6. What was the name of the restaurant hangout on *Saved by the Bell*?

7. What iconic five and dime store, that has a famous building in lower Manhattan named for it, went out of business in 1997? It later resurrected itself as Foot Locker.

8. What famous family of fireworks experts has been providing displays for nationwide extravaganzas since 1850? They have entertained at the inaugurations of Ronald Reagan, George H.W. Bush, Bill Clinton, and George W. Bush. For beer lovers, they went to Ireland to provide the pyrotechnics for the Guinness 250-year anniversary party.

9. Alphaville, Bob Dylan, and Rod Stewart all recorded a song with the same name. What was it?

10. In 1976, Betty Ford became the first First Lady to appear on a TV sitcom. On what show did she appear?

Answer Sheet

Everything & Anything
3 Rolls

Name_____

Answer Sheet

Everything & Anything
3 Rolls

Name_____

Answer Sheet

Everything & Anything
3 Rolls

Name_____

1.	1.	1.
2.	2.	2.
3.	3.	3.
4.	4.	4.
5.	5.	5.
6.	6.	6.
7.	7.	7.
8.	8.	8.
9.	9.	9.
10.	10.	10.

After you have filled out the sheet, fold your column underneath along the dashed line so the next restroom user won't see your answers. *The first player uses the far right column.*

Notes:

Notes:

Notes:

Television Sitcoms

 One Roll — Answers

1. *The Simpsons*. Debuting as part of *The Tracey Ullman Show* in 1987, or count it as its own in 1989.

2. Chocolate candies

3. Shoe salesman

4. Tony or Angela, depending on your interpretation

5. Ron Howard

6. Archie Bunker

7. To the moon

8. Alice, or the housekeeper

9. *Taxi*

10. *M*A*S*H* was based on the movie, which was based on the earlier novel, *MASH*, by Richard Hooker

Television Sitcoms

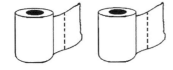 **Two Rolls — Answers**

1. Quahog, Rhode Island

2. *Laverne & Shirley*

3. *The Jeffersons* was a spinoff of *All in the Family*. Funny thing is, not all of the actors were the same. Look for a different Lionel in reruns depending on the day of the week.

4. *The Odd Couple*

5. *Alf*

6. *Family Matters*

7. *Happy Days*. His character's full name was Matsuo Takahashi. Arnold joked that he didn't have enough money to put his full name in lights outside of the restaurant.

8. Richard Nixon

9. Edna Garrett, Adelaide Brubaker, and Pearl Gallagher. Just the first names are fine.

10. Stanley Hudson

Television Sitcoms

Three Rolls — Answers

1. *Alice*

2. *Three's Company*

3. Norman Lear

4. *The Golden Girls*

5. Her grandmother

6. Five: Sondra, Denise, Theo, Vanessa, Rudy

7. Shelley Long

8. Emily, his wife from his old show, *The Bob Newhart Show*. It seems it was all a dream. Cop out? Well, many critics say it was one of the best finales ever written.

9. Behind the grandfather clock

10. *Out of This World*

Fads

 One Roll — Answers

1. *The Charleston*

2. Hula Hoop

3. Disco

4. Bell Bottoms

5. *The Macarena*

6. Lava Lamps. An ingenious design heats up wax so it's less dense than liquid. It then rises to the top, cools, and sinks to the bottom again.

7. Tickle Me Elmo

8. Ty Beanie Babies

9. Slinky

10. Frisbee. Walter Morrison's invention of the Pluto Platter was bought by Wham-O in 1957. The Frisbee was born.

Fads

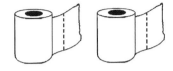 ## Two Rolls — Answers

1. Budweiser Beer from Anheuser-Busch

2. Pogs

3. Bubble gum

4. Pet Rocks

5. Grapefruit

6. Pagers or Beepers

7. Y2K

8. Freezy Freakies

9. Eight-Tracks, or Eight-Track Tapes

10. Dance Marathons

Fads

Three Rolls —
Answers

1. Garbage Pail Kids

2. Slap Bracelets

3. 54

4. Troll Dolls

5. Pole Sitting, or Flagpole Sitting. Kelly, and many copycats in the 1920s, would sit for days on a stool high atop a building. Kelly trained himself to sleep for ten minutes at a time. He had a contraption created with holes for his thumbs, so if he began to fall off his seat, he could catch himself. Kelly traded records with people until 1930, when Bill Penfield sat for 51 days, 20 hours in Iowa.

6. Flip-up sunglasses

7. Zoot Suit

8. Presto Magix, or Rub-on Transfers

9. Mood Ring

10. Kid Sister

Radio

 ## One Roll — Answers

1. Howard Stern

2. Federal Communications Commission (FCC)

3. Casey Kasem

4. Dick Clark

5. Orson Welles' *The War of the Worlds*. His Mercury Theater Production explicitly stated that it was not a real attack, but most listeners joined the show in progress. Some people were so panicked, they aimed shotguns at water towers confusing them for aliens.

6. *Good Morning, Vietnam*

7. George Carlin

8. Rush Limbaugh

9. *The Lone Ranger*. Tonto did not appear until the 12th episode.

10. XM Satellite Radio and Sirius Satellite Radio

Radio

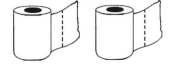 **Two Rolls — Answers**

1. Don Imus

2. National Public Radio (NPR)

3. Alan Freed. For taking bribes to play a band's music, Freed received a suspended sentence, and paid a $300 fine.

4. Dr. Laura Schlessinger

5. Seabiscuit defeated War Admiral

6. *WKRP*

7. Pittsburgh. Traditionally, stations east of the Mississippi River begin with the letter W. KDKA has been around longer than the rule. In its first broadcast, KDKA gave the results of the Presidential Election of 1920, where Warren G. Harding defeated James M. Cox. The announcers requested that if anyone was out there listening, they should send a letter confirming it.

8. Dr. Drew Pinsky, or Dr. Drew

9. Edward R. Murrow

10. *Video Killed the Radio Star* debuted just after midnight on August 1, 1981

Radio

Three Rolls — Answers

1. Freeman Gosden and Charles Correll

2. Tokyo Rose

3. WFAN in 1987

4. Jack Benny

5. Opie and Anthony

6. Mel Allen

7. Car Talk

8. *Talk Radio*. The movie was based on Colorado DJ Alan Berg, who was shot on his driveway by a neo-Nazi group member in 1984.

9. Amplitude Modulation and Frequency Modulation

10. Adam Curry

Famous People

 ## One Roll — Answers

1. Liza Minnelli

2. Paul Newman

3. Oprah Winfrey

4. Larry David

5. Barbra Streisand

6. Marlon Brando

7. George Clooney. Clooney also had bit parts on *Roseanne*, *The Golden Girls*, and *The Facts of Life*.

8. Keanu Reeves, and Alex Winter

9. Weird Al Yankovic

10. Ronald Reagan

Famous People

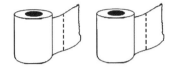 **Two Rolls — Answers**

1. Walter Cronkite

2. Jerry Lewis

3. Katharine Hepburn. She won four, including in 1934 for *Morning Glory*, and in 1982 for *On Golden Pond*.

4. Charlie Chaplin

5. Alec, Daniel, William (Billy), Stephen

6. Will Smith, or *The Fresh Prince*

7. Norma Jeane Mortensen at birth, changed to Norma Jeane Baker. If you just said Norma Jeane, count it.

8. Tom Hanks

9. Michael Caine and Jack Nicholson

10. Greta Garbo. Director and mentor Mauritz Stiller gave her this stage name in the early 1920s.

.

Famous People

Three Rolls — Answers

1. Seven. It's a trick question, because she was married eight times. She married Richard Burton twice. Others were: Conrad Hilton Jr., Michael Wilding, Michael Todd, Eddie Fisher, John Warner, and Larry Fotensky. So if you said eight, count it as a correct answer.

2. Rachael Ray

3. *Days of Our Lives*

4. Telly Savalas

5. Rudolph Valentino

6. In order of when they completed the achievement: Richard Rodgers (composer), Helen Hayes, Rita Moreno, John Gielgud, Audrey Hepburn, Marvin Hamlisch (composer), Jonathan Tunick (composer), Mel Brooks, Mike Nichols, Whoopi Goldberg, Barbra Streisand, and Liza Minelli.

7. *Once Bitten*

8. Billy Crystal, Whoopi Goldberg, and Robin Williams

9. David Letterman

10. Tom Cruise and Nicole Kidman. They were married soon after, and later starred together in *Far and Away* and *Eyes Wide Shut*.

Movies

 One Roll — Answers

1. *"One-Eyed" Willie*

2. *Rocky*

3. *Apocalypse Now*

4. *Rocky Horror Show* (the musical), and *The Rocky Horror Picture Show* (the film)

5. *The Wizard of Oz*. After extensively studying the film, most experts now believe that the object in question was an exotic bird that was moving while the actors danced down the Yellow Brick Road. For years, it was rumored to be a disgruntled Munchkin hanging himself. But the scene was filmed out of order before the Munchkins ever arrived on the set.

6. *Back To The Future*

7. *On the Waterfront*

8. Mike Tyson

9. *Airplane!*

10. Time travel

Movies

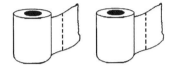

Two Rolls — Answers

1. Danny DeVito and Arnold Schwarzenegger

2. *Friday the 13th* has 11 sequels. *Halloween* has 9. *A Nightmare on Elm Street* has 8.

3. John F. Kennedy (for college football), Lyndon B. Johnson (for Vietnam heroism), and Richard M. Nixon (for ping pong)

4. *Pulp Fiction*

5. Estelle Reiner made that memorable order in *When Harry Met Sally*

6. *My Cousin Vinny*

7. Scott

8. Chocolate syrup. The movie was in black and white.

9. Bob Barker

10. The Stay Puft Marshmallow Man

Movies

Three Rolls — Answers

1. *Steamboat Willie* was the first released short of Mickey Mouse way back in 1928

2. *Gone with the Wind* (238 minutes). Then comes *The Ten Commandments* (220 minutes), *Ben Hur* (212 minutes), and *Titanic* (194 minutes).

3. Richard Donner

4. *Wings* won for 1927-1928

5. Henry Hill

6. Johnson

7. Amity Island

8. David O. Selznick. The Hays Office, which enforced the moral code, threatened a $5,000 fine.

9. Charlestown Chiefs

10. James Earl Jones

Food & Drink

 ## One Roll — Answers

1. Nathan's Famous. As of 2011, the record for most hot dogs consumed in the contest is 68 by Joey Chestnut.

2. 57

3. Michael Jackson

4. Bazooka Joe

5. Starbucks. The company was almost named Pequod, for the ship. Ultimately the store was named after the first mate of the ship, Starbuck.

6. Double Stuf Oreos

7. Snap, Crackle, and Pop!

8. Mr. Peanut of Planters Peanuts

9. Chef Boyardee. Boiardi spelled his name out phonetically so people could pronounce the brand.

10. Taco Bell

Food & Drink

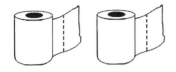 ## Two Rolls — Answers

1. Red. A food dye never used in the candy was suspected of being a carcinogen. To avoid confusing consumers, it was replaced by orange in 1976. Red made a comeback in 1987. It has been in packages ever since.

2. White Castle

3. Louisville, Kentucky

4. Classic

5. Samuel Adams

6. Hershey's Milk Chocolate Bar, Hershey's Special Dark, Mr. Goodbar, Krackel Bar

7. Hebrew National

8. 31

9. Gatorade was tested on the Florida Gators

10. Three

Food & Drink

 **Three Rolls —
Answers**

1. Willard Scott

2. Bingo

3. Ruth Cleveland, or Grover Cleveland's daughter. Although, the candy bar came out near the peak of Babe Ruth's career, he did not receive handsome royalties.

4. White Castle (1921), McDonald's (1940), Burger King (1953) Wendy's (1969)

5. Franken Berry and Boo Berry are still available usually around Halloween time. Yummy Mummy, and Fruit Brute can only be found in a cupboard that hasn't been cleaned out in decades.

6. Spam. It's true, there is a Hormel Spam Museum. They have cans stacked as far as the eye can see!

7. Fritos. The Frito Company would emerge from this recipe purchase. In 1961, the Frito Company merged with H.W. Lay's company to form Frito-Lay.

8. Subway. Frank DeLuca took a $1,000 loan from his friend Dr. Peter Buck. The first store opened in Bridgeport, Connecticut in 1965. Today, there are an estimated 35,000 stores in nearly 100 countries.

9. Wonder Bread. Originally, the bread even came with balloons. The logo was created by Elmer Cline. He was "wondered" by the sight of many colorful balloons in the International Balloon Race at the Indianapolis Motor Speedway in 1921.

10. Minute Maid

Music

 One Roll — Answers

1. Christie Brinkley

2. Tony Bennett

3. Michael Jackson's *Thriller*. Estimates of the sales vary. Some put them higher than 100 million albums. No other album comes close. Out of the nine songs on the album, seven were sold as singles. All seven were Top 10 hits on the *Billboard* Hot 100 chart.

4. *Appetite for Destruction* debuted in 1987, and was one of the strongest selling debut albums of all time

5. Cleveland, Ohio

6. Jimi Hendrix

7. Johnny Cash

8. Fab Morvan and Rob Pilatus, or Milli Vanilli. The true voices would form, "The Real Milli Vanilli" shortly after.

9. Bono

10. Sonny and Cher

Music

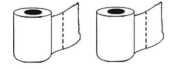 **Two Rolls — Answers**

1. The plane crash that killed Buddy Holly, Ritchie Valens, and The Big Bopper on February 3, 1959

2. Barry Manilow. He wrote many other jingles for companies including soft drinks Tab and Dr. Pepper. He has been honored at the Clio Awards.

3. Devo

4. *Slim Shady*

5. Natalie Cole sang with legendary singer Nat King Cole

6. Foo Fighters

7. Jimmy Page and Robert Plant

8. Aretha Franklin

9. Paris. Many fans have made the pilgrimage to Père Lachaise Cemetery where he is buried.

10. *Like a Virgin*

Music

Three Rolls — Answers

1. *Heartbreak Hotel* was released as a single, and went to Number One in 1956

2. Shawn Corey Carter

3. The Wallflowers

4. Velvet Revolver

5. Def Leppard. Rick Allen was injured before the *Hysteria* tour. He was still able to play using one arm, his legs, and an electronic drum. *Hysteria* sold even more copies than the group's previous album, *Pyromania*.

6. Phil Ochs

7. "Captain" Lou Albano

8. Martha and the Vandellas

9. The Traveling Wilburys

10. LeAnn Rimes

Games & Video Games

 ## One Roll — Answers

1. Boardwalk and Park Place

2. *Minesweeper*

3. *Pong*

4. Queen of Spades

5. *Mortal Kombat*

6. Ten points

7. Jenga

8. Cherry

9. Operation

10. *Tetris*

Games & Video Games

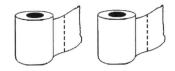 ## Two Rolls — Answers

1. Hungry Hungry Hippos

2. *Call of Duty*

3. Battleship

4. Taboo

5. A mushroom

6. Uno

7. Glass Joe

8. 8 x 8 = 64

9. *World of Warcraft*

10. *NBA Jam*

Games & Video Games

 **Three Rolls —
Answers**

1. Pinochle

2. *John Madden Football* was the title from 1988-1993

3. Sorry!

4. *Blades of Steel*

5. Mr. Green, Colonel Mustard, Mrs. Peacock, Professor Plum, Miss Scarlett, and Mrs. White

6. *Kaboom!*

7. Boggle

8. Game Gear

9. Four. Red, Blue, Yellow, Green

10. *The Legend of Zelda*

Game Shows

 ## One Roll — Answers

1. *The Price is Right* debuted on November 26, 1956. In 1972, the show took on its modern look as *The New Price is Right* (the new would later be dropped) hosted by Bob Barker. By the way, the host of the original show when it debuted was Bill Cullen. At that time, Barker was hosting *Truth or Consequences*.

2. *Who Wants to Be a Millionaire*

3. Merv Griffin

4. A *Whammy*

5. Monty Hall would go through the audience during the end credits of *Let's Make a Deal*. A good reason to attend the taping with a box of paper clips in your pocket!

6. Richard Dawson

7. *Are You Smarter Than a Fifth Grader?*

8. Ken Jennings. He won 74 *Jeopardy!* games in a row, and made $2.52 million. He won over a million more in other game show appearances, including *Are You Smarter Than a 5th Grader?*, *1 vs. 100*, *Grand Slam*, and subsequent appearances on *Jeopardy!* Grand Total: As of 2011, over $3.5 million.

9. People were trying to *Win Ben Stein's Money*

10. *The Newlywed Game*

Game Shows

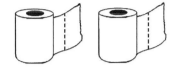 **Two Rolls — Answers**

1. Art Fleming. Trebek took over in 1984.

2. *The Gong Show*

3. Twenty

4. Brian Dunkleman

5. *To Tell the Truth*

6. Betty White

7. *Cash Cab*

8. *Tic-Tac-Dough*

9. *Win, Lose or Draw*

10. R, S, T, L, N, E

Game Shows

Three Rolls — Answers

1. In 1980 Vanna ran down to contestant's row on *The Price is Right*

2. Jim J. Bullock

3. $300

4. *The Sundae Slide*. It was usually saturated with some type of chocolate syrup or pudding.

5. Charles Van Doren. Stempel needed to identify the Best Picture of 1955 (*Marty*), but answered with 1954's Best Picture (*On the Waterfront*).

6. Brett Somers (87 years-old) and Charles Nelson Reilly (76 years old)

7. Twenty-six, meaning you have a less than a 4% chance of winning the big number if you go all the way

8. *The Weakest Link*

9. Gene Rayburn

10. *Sale of the Century*

Everything & Anything

 ## One Roll — Answers

1. *Little Shop of Horrors*

2. Costco. The two merged in 1993 and became PriceCostco. In 1997, it became Costco.

3. Groovy. Groovy is a modification of groove, which was a term used in both jazz and swing music from the 1920s and 1930s.

4. Polaroid Instant Camera

5. Home Box Office

6. *Rolling Stone*. The picture was taken just hours before Lennon was assassinated on December 8, 1980.

7. Salsa

8. Memphis Zoo, San Diego Zoo, US National Zoo in Washington, DC, Zoo Atlanta

9. Stephen King

10. Universal Studios, Orlando

Everything & Anything

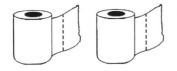 **Two Rolls — Answers**

1. Maytag

2. Magic Kingdom Park, Epcot, Disney's Hollywood Studios, Disney's Animal Kingdom Park

3. The Bob

4. Swanson. The first dinner they marketed in 1953 was a replica of Thanksgiving Dinner, complete with turkey, peas, sweet potatoes, and corn bread dressing. Swanson's Gerry Thomas gets the credit for inventing it.

5. *Sports Illustrated*

6. *Cats.* It closed with 7,485 performances in 2000 after an 18-year run. *The Phantom of the Opera* eclipsed it in 2006, and is currently still playing on Broadway with over 10,000 performances.

7. Michigan Stadium, or "The Big House." The seating capacity is 109,901.

8. California (Lakewood to be exact). The first Denny's was known as Danny's Donuts.

9. Coney Island, New York. It was quite dangerous, caused neck injuries, and quickly closed down.

10. Mr. Whipple

Everything & Anything

 **Three Rolls —
Answers**

1. *The Gooch*

2. Licorice. Thomas Adams put the flavor into Black Jack Chewing Gum, which was also the first gum to come in sticks.

3. Six Flags Great Adventure in New Jersey. The coaster is called *Kingda Ka*. It goes from 0 to 128 mph in just 3.5 seconds, and travels 45 stories. It is also the fastest coaster in North America.

4. Ralph Lauren

5. Gobots

6. "The Max"

7. Woolworth. They became Venator Group, and then Foot Locker

8. The Grucci Family

9. *Forever Young*. Bob Dylan released it in 1974. Alphaville in 1984. Rod Stewart's 1988 version was so similar to the 1974 song, that he now has to split the royalties with Dylan.

10. *The Mary Tyler Moore Show*. The First Lady called Mary on the phone. Mary thought it was a joke, and told the caller that her Betty Ford impression needed some work.

Scorecard — Name: _____

Category	# Right		# of Pts.		Tot. Pts.
Television Sitcoms - 1 Roll		x	1	=	
Television Sitcoms - 2 Rolls		x	2	=	
Television Sitcoms - 3 Rolls		x	3	=	
Fads - 1 Roll		x	1	=	
Fads - 2 Rolls		x	2	=	
Fads - 3 Rolls		x	3	=	
Radio - 1 Roll		x	1	=	
Radio - 2 Rolls		x	2	=	
Radio - 3 Rolls		x	3	=	
Famous People - 1 Roll		x	1	=	
Famous People - 2 Rolls		x	2	=	
Famous People - 3 Rolls		x	3	=	
Movies - 1 Roll		x	1	=	
Movies - 2 Rolls		x	2	=	
Movies - 3 Rolls		x	3	=	
Food & Drink - 1 Roll		x	1	=	
Food & Drink - 2 Rolls		x	2	=	
Food & Drink - 3 Rolls		x	3	=	
Music - 1 Roll		x	1	=	
Music - 2 Rolls		x	2	=	
Music - 3 Rolls		x	3	=	
Games & Video Games - 1 Roll		x	1	=	
Games & Video Games - 2 Rolls		x	2	=	
Games & Video Games - 3 Rolls		x	3	=	
Game Shows - 1 Roll		x	1	=	
Game Shows - 2 Rolls		x	2	=	
Game Shows - 3 Rolls		x	3	=	
Everything & Anything - 1 Roll		x	1	=	
Everything & Anything - 2 Rolls		x	2	=	
Everything & Anything - 3 Rolls		x	3	=	

Grand Total

Scorecard — Name: _____

Category	# Right		# of Pts.		Tot. Pts.
Television Sitcoms - 1 Roll		x	1	=	
Television Sitcoms - 2 Rolls		x	2	=	
Television Sitcoms - 3 Rolls		x	3	=	
Fads - 1 Roll		x	1	=	
Fads - 2 Rolls		x	2	=	
Fads - 3 Rolls		x	3	=	
Radio - 1 Roll		x	1	=	
Radio - 2 Rolls		x	2	=	
Radio - 3 Rolls		x	3	=	
Famous People - 1 Roll		x	1	=	
Famous People - 2 Rolls		x	2	=	
Famous People - 3 Rolls		x	3	=	
Movies - 1 Roll		x	1	=	
Movies - 2 Rolls		x	2	=	
Movies - 3 Rolls		x	3	=	
Food & Drink - 1 Roll		x	1	=	
Food & Drink - 2 Rolls		x	2	=	
Food & Drink - 3 Rolls		x	3	=	
Music - 1 Roll		x	1	=	
Music - 2 Rolls		x	2	=	
Music - 3 Rolls		x	3	=	
Games & Video Games - 1 Roll		x	1	=	
Games & Video Games - 2 Rolls		x	2	=	
Games & Video Games - 3 Rolls		x	3	=	
Game Shows - 1 Roll		x	1	=	
Game Shows - 2 Rolls		x	2	=	
Game Shows - 3 Rolls		x	3	=	
Everything & Anything - 1 Roll		x	1	=	
Everything & Anything - 2 Rolls		x	2	=	
Everything & Anything - 3 Rolls		x	3	=	

Grand Total

Scorecard — Name: _____

Category	# Right		# of Pts.		Tot. Pts.
Television Sitcoms - 1 Roll		x	1	=	
Television Sitcoms - 2 Rolls		x	2	=	
Television Sitcoms - 3 Rolls		x	3	=	
Fads - 1 Roll		x	1	=	
Fads - 2 Rolls		x	2	=	
Fads - 3 Rolls		x	3	=	
Radio - 1 Roll		x	1	=	
Radio - 2 Rolls		x	2	=	
Radio - 3 Rolls		x	3	=	
Famous People - 1 Roll		x	1	=	
Famous People - 2 Rolls		x	2	=	
Famous People - 3 Rolls		x	3	=	
Movies - 1 Roll		x	1	=	
Movies - 2 Rolls		x	2	=	
Movies - 3 Rolls		x	3	=	
Food & Drink - 1 Roll		x	1	=	
Food & Drink - 2 Rolls		x	2	=	
Food & Drink - 3 Rolls		x	3	=	
Music - 1 Roll		x	1	=	
Music - 2 Rolls		x	2	=	
Music - 3 Rolls		x	3	=	
Games & Video Games - 1 Roll		x	1	=	
Games & Video Games - 2 Rolls		x	2	=	
Games & Video Games - 3 Rolls		x	3	=	
Game Shows - 1 Roll		x	1	=	
Game Shows - 2 Rolls		x	2	=	
Game Shows - 3 Rolls		x	3	=	
Everything & Anything - 1 Roll		x	1	=	
Everything & Anything - 2 Rolls		x	2	=	
Everything & Anything - 3 Rolls		x	3	=	

Grand Total

How did you do?

500 +   — King/Queen of the Throne

400-499 — Topper of the Hopper

350-399 — Porcelain Prince/Princess

300-349 — Toileterrific!

250-299 — Keep Flushing for the Stars

200-249 — Might Need a Plunger

150-199 — Gotta call the Plumber

Below 150 — Clogged

Try a different Toiletrivia Book!

Made in the USA
Lexington, KY
06 December 2011